YOU AND RHYTHM

A Handbook of Rhythm Activities for the Elementary School Classroom

Mary E. Johnson, Ph.D.
Jo Ellen Thompson Clow, M.Mus.Ed.
Stephen H. Barnes, Ph.D.

UNIVERSITY
PRESS OF
AMERICA

LANHAM • NEW YORK • LONDON

TABLE OF CONTENTS

iii

LEARNING GAMES (cont'd)

PREFACE

Natural rhythms, large and small, surround us: vast galactic cycles, the orbiting of our planet Earth, and the comforting familiarity of seasonal and day/night alternations. We watch tides and civilizations rise and fall. As individuals we live among a fascinating web of periodicities. We work and rest, leave home and return, think and act; we breathe in and out, have a systolic and diastolic heart, we walk (L R, L R) and we waltz (L R L, R L R). Our songs and dances reflect the pleasure of responding to rhythmic patterns. Thus our lives tell us much about rhythm as a fluid, energizing, organizing force.

Although sometimes we think of RHYTHM only as a musical term, a sense of rhythm is not limited to a musical context. There is social timing and sports timing. People who function well in groups sense the rhythm of the situation, and many work skills depend on rhythmic finesse.

As teachers, we want our students to have this harmony of body, mind, and emotion that is "a sense of rhythm." Rhythm games are the most natural starting point, since rhythmic development in youngsters is best approached through bodily movement.

With this approach in mind, the authors have developed *YOU AND RHYTHM,* a compilation of over forty challenging, amusing, and varied rhythm activities for the elementary school classroom.

This handbook has been influenced by the ideas of Emile Jaques-Dalcroze, whose work is uniquely valuable in exploring the connections among bodily movement, intellection, and rhythm. His system is known as Dalcroze eurhythmics. Some readers will have already noted the pun on the term *eurhythmics* in this handbook's title.

The authors of this book are particularly grateful to Dr. Robert Abramson of the Manhattan School of Music for his dedicated eurhythmic expertise. His efforts have been a major factor in keeping Dalcroze eurhythmics a vigorous and viable part of the American educational scene. Some of the activities in *YOU AND RHYTHM* have been adapted from the eurhythmic exercises used in workshops conducted by Dr. Abramson. To him this handbook is happily and respectfully dedicated.

In using these games with your students, you will discover both the joys and the benefits of rhythmic motion. The results of this kind of rhythmic experience show very quickly with young children, not just in improved physical coordination and balance but also in focused attention, in memory skills, and in group awareness. This handbook may also be used at home by parents of children between roughly five and twelve years of age.

The book was designed to be used successfully by teachers and parents regardless of musical training; the games-format was developed specifically with this in mind. Please read the section HOW TO USE THIS HANDBOOK carefully, see the GLOSSARY OF SYMBOLS, and think through the first three games in order. Then you are ready for eurhythmic learning and eurhythmic fun with your youngsters.

HOW TO USE THIS HANDBOOK

YOU AND RHYTHM presents forty-one rhythm games (most with variations) appropriate for use in the elementary school and in other settings involving youngsters ages five to twelve. The actions in these games (listening, speaking, moving, and improvising) are based on the ability to perceive, react to, and create upon the framework of a steady beat or pulse. The games have been kept very simple with a minimum of props: no drum, piano, or record player is needed.

Sixteen of these activities are contained in the first section of the book, LIVELY GAMES/QUIET GAMES. As the title suggests, these activities can be conducted in either a brisk or a relaxed fashion. Each game can be used to revitalize a group after a long period of inactivity or as a quieting game following vigorous activity. Twenty-five LEARNING GAMES comprise the second section of the handbook. Here basic concepts in arithmetic, geometry, spelling, poetry, and the visual arts are reinforced by employing a rhythmic concept: the steady beat or pulse. The maintenance of a steady pulse is the most crucial aspect in fostering the rhythmic development of children.

The first three games are plotted not only as simple "fun" activities but also as a sequential introduction to the format and procedures of the entire collection of games. Before you begin these games with your class, please take time to go through this process:

Walk, in a free and natural way.

Think of your steps as: *   *   *   *   *   *etc.*

You could say, as you walk: STEP   STEP   STEP   STEP   STEP   *etc.*

Or you could say: LEFT   RIGHT   LEFT   RIGHT   LEFT   *etc.*

Listen to a clock tick.

Think of the ticks as: *   *   *   *   *   *etc.*

You could say: TICK   TICK   TICK   TICK   TICK   *etc.*

Take your pulse.

Think of those heartbeats as: *   *   *   *   *   *etc.*

You could say: BEAT   BEAT   BEAT   BEAT   BEAT   *etc.*

Now, just <u>think</u> the beats
*   instead of walking or*
*   speaking them:*   (*)   (*)   (*)   (*)   (*)   *etc.*

Notice the momentum set up by these equally-spaced "beats" in time.
They set up the expectation of the pattern's going on and on, in a
springy and satisfying rhythm.

In these games, the equally-spaced asterisks represent steady, equally-spaced beats. And, as in reading words, the continuum of beats (pulses) may be read in successive lines, left to right, as:

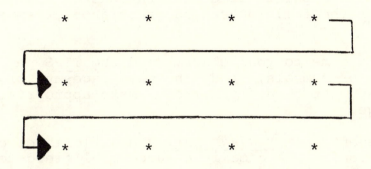

In these games, the row of asterisks at the top of a game page is setting up this beat framework for the whole game.

The pace (tempo or speed) of these beats might vary from one playing of a game to the next or from game to game (based on its objectives and/or the teacher's directions). However, at whatever speed, it is absolutely essential that the teacher establish a steady beat upon which to play the game.

Each game in this book begins with a TIPS page alerting the teacher to certain aspects of the activity immediately following; these might include the physical conditions to be met to start the activity, the objectives of the game, suggested teacher explanations for the class, and/or recommendations for minor variations in the game. Space is provided on this page also for the personal/professional notes of the teacher. Following the TIPS page is the game page, which utilizes the beat-format previously discussed.

Please note that the last item to appear on most game pages suggests possible variations of the activity just presented. This is abbreviated as VAR or VARS. These serve to spark the teacher's imagination in solidifying, extending, or amplifying the actions or concepts presented in the game itself. Most describe more sophisticated realizations of the games and should be attempted <u>after</u> the fully-presented games above them are mastered.

Before presenting a game to your class, read the <u>TIPS</u> page, check the <u>GLOSSARY</u> for the use of symbols, study the game page and practice any needed gestures. You may want to use a mirror. Make appropriate notes for yourself on the <u>TIPS</u> page.

The activities presented in *YOU AND RHYTHM* are flexible, encouraging invention and improvisation. Each game is a successful field-tested <u>model</u> which the teacher can build upon, adapt, or modify. Be flexible, inventive, and creative--and always keep the beat steady.

GLOSSARY OF SYMBOLS

T   The teacher.

Ss   The students.

S   An individual student.

*   The steady beat or pulse upon which the activity (spoken words or actions) is based.

(*)   A silent, felt beat or pulse kept in the minds of the game players.

\#   Indicates that the line or section may be repeated at the discretion of the teacher.

etc.   Suggests teacher option in developing additional gestures or words along the same lines as presented in the game.

VAR/VARS   Ideas for extending the game.

Italicized directions are for T and Ss' actions.

Non-italicized directions denote <u>spoken</u> words of the teacher used to begin a game or change the action during the course of a game.

BEAT, BOOM, etc., game words presented without parentheses, are to be spoken to the steady beat.

CLAP, TAP, WALK, STAMP, JUMP, etc., action words presented without parentheses, indicate a combination of the action with the spoken word.

(SNAP), (NOD), (POINT), (STEP), etc., action words within parentheses, indicate an action without the spoken word.

LIVELY GAMES/QUIET GAMES

Tips for HERE'S MY BEAT

This game shows that there is an ongoing beat (a pulse) inside everyone.

Discuss the heartbeat with the class before playing the game.

After the Ss are confident with HERE'S MY BEAT, you may wish to discuss other recurring beat patterns in their experience, e.g., walking, clocks ticking, breathing, the pattern of seasons, etc. Point out those patterns which are strictly repetitious and those which contain some differentiation. For instance, walking is STEP STEP STEP STEP, and also LEFT RIGHT LEFT RIGHT; breathing alternates "inhale" with "exhale."

You may want to emphasize (accent) the first pulse in each line in these games.

YOUR NOTES

HERE'S MY BEAT

	*	*	*	*	
T takes own wrist pulse or that of a student and reports the steady beat to the class, saying:	BEAT	BEAT	BEAT	BEAT	#
Have the Ss join in:	BEAT	BEAT	BEAT	BEAT	#
Change the word:	BOOM	BOOM	BOOM	BOOM	#
Clap and say it:	CLAP	CLAP	CLAP	CLAP	#
Find different ways:	(SNAP)	(SNAP)	(SNAP)	(SNAP)	#
or	(NOD)	(NOD)	(NOD)	(NOD)	#
or	(POINT)	(POINT)	(POINT)	(POINT)	#
or	(STEP)	(STEP) *(in place)*	(STEP)	(STEP)	

etc.

VAR: Divide the Ss into pairs or small groups so everyone can experience taking a pulse and showing the beat as above (clap, snap, nod, etc.)

VAR: Base the game on a student's pulse taken after some lively activity (recess or gym). Contrast it with the beat taken after a rest period.

Tips for <u>CATCH THE BEAT</u>

Steady beats are infectious. In this game the Ss explore "catching" the beat from you. Ask them to echo your four-beat pattern. Remind the class to listen to the entire pattern before responding.

Please note that the third variation involves catching the pace of the beat rather than echoing each line. Try speaking a familiar poem faster or slower than you would ordinarily. Keep the beat steady!

<u>YOUR NOTES</u>

CATCH THE BEAT

```
                                   *        *        *        *
T:  Catch my beat!              (CLAP)   (CLAP)   (CLAP)   (CLAP)
                                       (repeat the line if necessary)

Ss respond, echoing:            (CLAP)   (CLAP)   (CLAP)   (CLAP)
                                       (repeat the teacher's pattern)

T changes the action:           (SNAP)   (SNAP)   (SNAP)   (SNAP)      #

Ss respond, echoing:            (SNAP)   (SNAP)   (SNAP)   (SNAP)      #
```

*Find different ways to make the four-beat pattern (nod, tap, pat, etc.),
Ss echoing each action.*

VAR: Ss work in pairs, one giving and one catching the beat.

VAR: T sets beat and calls on individuals to respond.

VAR: "Catch the beat" with a poem, for example:

```
                                   *        *        *        *

T claps and speaks, Ss join in:  ROW      ROW      ROW   your BOAT

                                 GENT  -ly DOWN   the STREAM      (*)
                                             (clap, but no word)
                                 MER-ri-ly MER-ri-ly MER-ri-ly MER-ri-ly

                                 LIFE    is BUT      a  DREAM      (*)
```

5

Tips for <u>CHANGE THE BEAT-KEEPER</u>

This is an improvisational game which explores different ways to keep an established beat going. Let the Ss experiment along with you.

As you change the beat-keeper, keep the pulse steady.

<u>YOUR NOTES</u>

CHANGE THE BEAT-KEEPER

		*	*	*	*	
T:	Here's my beat--tap along with me.	(TAP)	(TAP)	(TAP)	(TAP)	#
	I'm going to change the beat-keeper: *(keep the beat steady)*	(CLUCK) *(tongue)*	(CLUCK)	(CLUCK)	(CLUCK)	#
	Here's another way:	(NOD)	(NOD)	(NOD)	(NOD)	#
	Make up another way yourself:	(*) *(all different in the class)*	(*)	(*)	(*)	#
	Let's all do Susie's beat-keeper:	(*) *(Susie's way)*	(*)	(*)	(*)	#
	Mike, give us another way:	(*) *(Mike's way)*	(*)	(*)	(*)	#
					etc.	

_____

VARS: Experiment with different kinds of changes. Here are a few ideas:

Change the KIND of sound: rap on desk, finger-clap, scrape foot, etc.
Change the AMOUNT of sound: soft to loud, loud to soft.
Change from SOUNDS (claps, etc.) to SILENCE (nods, swing arms, etc.)
Change the LOCALE of beat-keeper: clap high, clap low; left, right, etc.
Change the TOTAL SPACE of the beat-keepers: tiny gestures, huge gestures.
Change the NUMBER of beats in the pattern: use a 3-beat or 5-beat pattern.
Change WHO is keeping the beat: T alternating with Ss; individuals down
   the rows; boys as a group alternating with girls, etc.

<u>Tips for THE CHESHIRE CAT BEAT</u>

Like the cat in <u>Alice in Wonderland</u>, the beat appears and disappears in
this game. Think the beat very strongly and let it appear as you talk.

Students imitate your actions as they see the beat appear.

<u>YOUR NOTES</u>

THE CHESHIRE CAT BEAT

	*	*	*	*	

T: I have a Chessy Cat beat inside
    me, but it doesn't show!

    I can certainly feel it, though.
    You help me feel it too.   (*)   (*)   (*)   (*)   #

    Watch, now it's beginning
    to show, just in my finger: (BEAT) (BEAT) (BEAT) (BEAT)   #
      (show beat; Ss join in)   *etc.*

    Just in my toes:
    Now in my shoulder:
    Now my head:
    Now it's moving my whole body--
    But it's disappearing again:
      (progressively smaller gestures)
    Just in my left elbow:
    Just in my nose:
    Now you can't see it:
      (no visible gestures)
    But it's still there:
    In your eyebrow:
      (T selects S; beat reappears)
    In your shoelace:
      (T points to second student, etc.)
    Now it's all gone. Goodbye, Chessy Cat!
      (Beat disappears for last time)

VARS: Let individual Ss show where the beat is, the class imitating.
       Have the beat pass from S to S.
       Have the beat disappear in the exact order (body parts) in which
          it appears.

9

Tips for STEP-WALK-RUN

This game involves larger movement and needs more space than the previous games. The easiest formation is a circle, but the game can be adapted to several small circles or a double circle. You could use a straight line or double line, moving forward and back across the room.

Your words and your actions cue the changes of motion. Be very definite.

YOUR NOTES

STEP-WALK-RUN

*　　　　　　　*　　　　　　　*　　　　　　　*

Ss form a circle.

T: I have a beat in my feet!
    Watch, and do it with me: (STEP)   (STEP)   (STEP)   (STEP)   #
                                    (T and Ss step in place)

    Now say it too: STEP   STEP   STEP   STEP   #

    Now everyone walk, this way: (WALK)   (WALK)   (WALK)   (WALK)   #
                                    (T directs clockwise motion of circle)

    Now let's run!   (RUN - run) (RUN - run) (RUN - run) (RUN - run) #
             (T shows two running steps to each beat)

————————————————

VAR: After doing the game in the order above, reverse the order to end quietly,
      stepping in place.

VAR: To continue the game, T cues any one of the three actions (stepping,
      walking, running) in random order.

VAR: At some point in the game, T signals STOP! Ss freeze, but the feel of the
      beat goes on. The previous action resumes when T signals GO! The stopped
      beats may be kept by voice, gesture, or just in the imagination.

VAR: Change the mood of the game. Begin like a march, a sleepy doll, or an
      elephant, etc. The pace should change to fit the mood.

VAR: Step, walk, and run backwards in the circle (be careful).

VAR: Improvise other actions (jump, gallop, tip-toe, hop, etc.).

Tips for A CHANGE OF CHARACTER

Before playing this game, again consider both the amount of space available
and the number of students to be involved. Form the students into one
large circle or several smaller circles. With this game especially,
consider selecting a small demonstration group to play, eventually
involving all members of the class.

YOUR NOTES

A CHANGE OF CHARACTER

	*	*	*	*	
T sets beat, walking and speaking:	WALK	WALK	WALK	WALK	#
Ss join in:	WALK	WALK	WALK	WALK	#
T directs change of beat-keeping:	STAMP	STAMP	STAMP	STAMP	#

(keep the beat steady)

TIP	-	TOE	TIP	-	TOE	#
JUMP		JUMP	JUMP		JUMP	#
GI - ant	STEP,	GI - ant	STEP			#
TI - ny	STEP,	TI - ny	STEP			#

etc.

———————————

VAR: T cues the new action visually with no verbal direction.

VAR: Ss take turns as leader, directing change in action.

13

Tips for <u>SNAPPER</u>

This game is useful when you have some extra unplanned minutes. The
Ss may be sitting or standing. Try <u>SNAPPER</u> when your students are waiting
in bus lines or lunch lines.

<u>YOUR NOTES</u>

SNAPPER

	*	*	*	*	
T sets the beat by snapping *fingers (both hands):*	(SNAP)	(SNAP)	(SNAP)	(SNAP)	#
Ss join in:	(SNAP)	(SNAP)	(SNAP)	(SNAP)	#
					etc.

Continuing the beat--
    snap four beats to one side of body,
    then four beats to the other:

    snap high/snap low, four beats each:

    alternate low and high, two beats each:

    alternate R and L hands:

    move both hands in the same direction:

    move hands in opposite directions:

    use patterns like R R R L, etc.:

    use only one hand:

    alternate one hand with both hands, etc.

VAR: Try patterns using silence on a beat: (SNAP)   (*)   (SNAP)   (SNAP), etc.

VAR: Ss take turns being the leader.

VAR: Use a different beat-keeper (clap, pat, nod, etc.)

15

Tips for <u>WIGWAG</u>

How many two-beat alternating-gesture patterns can you improvise? Dozens!
This game outlines just a few to get you started.

The cues are visual.

Repeat a pattern until most Ss are successfully involved; change before
boredom sets in.

The "wigwag" gesture comes from semaphore signaling. Make fists as if you
were holding signal flags. Start with the left arm fully extended to the
left side, right elbow bent so that the fist is in front of the chest. On
the beat, swing both arms down to the right, ending with the right arm
extended and the left fist in front of the chest. Alternate these positions
crisply on the beats.

<u>YOUR NOTES</u>

WIGWAG

		*		*	
T makes these gestures to a					
two-beat pattern and Ss imitate--					
arms:	(WIG	–	WAG)		#
shoulders:	(UP	–	DOWN)		#
head:	(CHIN UP	–	CHIN DOWN)		#
eyes:	(TO RIGHT	–	TO LEFT)		#
face:	(SMILE	–	FROWN)		#
hands:	(HIGH	–	LOW)		#
one foot:	(LIFT IT	–	STAMP!)		#
					etc.

VAR: Request S improvisations.

VAR: Say a word with each gesture:

CLAP	–	SNAP	#
or			
YES!	–	NO!	#
(quick nod)		*(quick shake of head)*	

*	*	*	

VAR: Try a three-beat pattern:

(CLAP)	(SNAP)	(SNAP)	#
or			
(SNAP)	(HOP)	(HOP)	#

17

Tips for HEAD AND SHOULDERS

An attention-getter at any grade level, HEAD AND SHOULDERS is easily
employed in the early primary grades for the learning of body parts.

YOUR NOTES

HEAD AND SHOULDERS

	*	*	*	*	
T touches the named body part on each beat and with the Ss joining in, says:	HEAD	HEAD	HEAD	HEAD	#
	EYE	EYE	EYE	EYE	#
	SHOULD-er	SHOULD-er	SHOULD-er	SHOULD-er	#
	KNEE	KNEE	KNEE	KNEE	#

etc.

VAR: T says the word on the first
beat; Ss touch that part on
2nd, 3rd, and 4th beat: NOSE   (TOUCH)   (TOUCH)   (TOUCH)   #
                          or
                           ELBOW   (TOUCH)   (TOUCH)   (TOUCH)   #

VAR: Alternate the body parts
to be named and touched: HEAD   SHOULD-er HEAD   SHOULD-er   #

VAR: Point instead of touch: TIM   (POINT)   (POINT)   (POINT)   #

VAR: Play the game silently, with Ss getting visual cues from T or from a
student leader.

VAR: Use classroom objects (desk, chair, book, pencil, etc.)

VAR: Use a three-beat pattern (heel - toe - toe, etc.)

19

Tips for <u>MAKE-BELIEVE</u>

This game encourages imaginative thinking. Ss may lie on the floor or place their heads on their desks.

<u>YOUR NOTES</u>

MAKE-BELIEVE

T: Make believe you are Tom
Sawyer floating on a raft
down a wide river. You
can feel the raft moving   *   *   *   *
with the steady flow of
the river. Listen to the
sound of the waves: SPLISH   SPLASH   SPLISH   SPLASH   #

Now let's say it together: SPLISH   SPLASH   SPLISH   SPLASH   #

Feel the beat in your
fingertips as we say it: SPLISH   SPLASH   SPLISH   SPLASH   #

Now without saying anything,
tap the beat with your
fingertips: (TAP)   (TAP)   (TAP)   (TAP)   #

Now let's keep the beat
inside our heads: (*)   (*)   (*)   (*)   #

Let's say it again: SPLISH   SPLASH   SPLISH   SPLASH   #

We're so relaxed now; let's stop the raft and rest.

VAR: Proceed with further make-believe images. For instance, T says, "As
we're floating, feel the warmth of the sun, hear the croaking of the
frogs," etc.

VAR: Develop holiday ideas involving ghosts, snowflakes, Indians, pumpkins, etc.

VAR: Do the activity with a quicker pace for energizing the class.

21

Tips for <u>HAMMER AND NAIL I</u>

This begins as a teacher-initiated call-and-response game.

The actions in <u>HAMMER AND NAIL</u> can be vigorous or gentle, fast or slow, but let a definite beat control each segment of the game.

Let individual Ss improvise the call as soon as they're ready.

<u>YOUR NOTES</u>

HAMMER AND NAIL I

                    *   *   *   *

T says: HERE'S a HAM-mer   DRIV-ing a NAIL--

T and Ss rap on desks: (POUND)   (POUND)   (POUND)   (POUND)

T makes a question of line one: HOW does a HAM-mer   DRIVE   a NAIL?

T and Ss rap on desks: (POUND)   (POUND)   (POUND)   (POUND)   #
                                                         etc.

VAR: Extend the game with another question and rhymed answer. For instance,
      add the following to HAMMER AND NAIL:

T says: WHY does a HAM-mer   DRIVE   a NAIL?

T and Ss rap on desks: (POUND)   (POUND)   (POUND)   (POUND)

T makes a rhyme with line one: MAK-ing a MAIL-box   FOR   the MAIL.

T and Ss rap on desks: (POUND)   (POUND)   (POUND)   (POUND)

23

Tips for <u>HAMMER AND NAIL II</u>

Here are some other possibilities using the call-and-response concept introduced in <u>HAMMER AND NAIL I</u>.

Use your imagination, too, for more variations.

<u>YOUR NOTES</u>

HAMMER AND NAIL II

	*	*	*	*
T says:	HEAR the WIND on	a WIN-ter	NIGHT--	
Ss respond, saying:	WHOOOoooo (*)	WHOOOoooo	(*)	
T says:	WHAT does a WIN-ter	WIND	SAY?	
Ss respond, saying:	WHOOOoooo (*)	WHOOOoooo	(*)	

_____

T says:	HERE is SUS -an	EAT-ing a	PIZ-za--
Ss respond, saying:	YUMmmmm (*)	YUMmmmm	(*)
T says:	WOULD you LIKE to	EAT a	PIZ-za?
Ss respond, saying:	YESssss! (*)	YESssss!	(*)

_____

T says:	HERE'S a CLOCK	TICK-ing a - WAY--
Ss respond, saying:	TICK TOCK	TICK TOCK
T says:	WHAT does a TICK-ing	CLOCK SAY?
Ss respond, saying:	TICK TOCK	TICK TOCK #

etc.

Tips for <u>WIND-UP/WIND-DOWN</u>

In this game, the students pretend to be wind-up toys. As the game nears its
end, the beat slows down.

<u>WIND-UP/WIND-DOWN</u> can be used to revitalize a class after a long period of
inactivity, or as a quieting game following vigorous activity. To begin
this game, let the students mime a toy very much in need of winding.

<u>YOUR NOTES</u>

WIND-UP/WIND-DOWN

	*		*		*		*	
T "winds-up" Ss to establish beat:	WIND	-	UP,	WIND	-	UP,		#
T adds the name of a toy:	RO	-	BOT,	RO	-	BOT,		#
	BE	a	RO-bot,	BE	a	RO-bot		#
	BE	a	RO-bot,	BE	a	RO-bot		#
Ss move to the beat in the character of the toy. As the "toy" begins to wind-down, the beat gradually slows:	WIND	-	DOWN,	WIND	-	DOWN		#
To end the game:	NOW		FALL	DOWN!		(*)		
						(silence)		

VAR: Use different toys: Toy Soldier (march-like actions), Toy Mouse (scurrying on all fours), Merry-GO-Round (up-and-down gestures in place), etc.

VAR: Select an individual student or small group(s) to act out game.

Tips for <u>I'M GIVING YOU A PRESENT</u>

In this game, an imaginary object is passed rhythmically from student to student around a circle. Students may be standing or sitting.

To begin, T stands in the middle of the circle. Before speaking, T shows the beat by dipping cupped hands in a steady rhythm. All Ss should imitate this gesture and keep it going as a help to the gesture of actually "passing it on."

The first time you play this game, help the object to be passed on the correct beat by clasping the cupped hands of the passer between your hands, reinforcing the gesture of transferral to the next Ss's hands.

"ON" is the action word for the transfer, until the Ss become adept. When it gets easy you can transfer on the word "PASS", in other words, on every beat.

This game is an adaptation of "Passing the Ball," one of the eurhythmic exercises developed by Dr. Robert Abramson of the Manhattan School of Music.

<u>YOUR NOTES</u>

I'M GIVING YOU A PRESENT

                          *   *   *   *

T mimes taking an object from
desk or pocket and sets the   I'm GIV-ing   YOU   a PRE   -   SENT,
beat, saying:

                                    a PRE   -   SENT, a PRE   -   SENT.

Ss imitate the beat gesture,
joining T in saying: I'm GIV-ing   YOU   a PRE   -   SENT,

                                    PLEASE   PASS it ON!   (*)
                                            (T transfers "object" to S)

                                    PASS   PASS   PASS   it ON!   #
                                            (S transfers "object" to next S)

Repeat around the circle until
T is ready for faster action: PASS   it ON!   PASS it ON!   #
                                        (transfer)   (transfer)

                                    PASS   PASS   PASS   PASS   #
                                (transfer)(transfer)(transfer)(transfer)

VAR: Name the present, changing the quality of the gesture to match, e.g.,

                I'm GIV-ing   YOU   a FEA   -   THER, etc.
                I'm GIV-ing   YOU   a CORN -   FLAKE, etc.

VAR: Use a real object (eraser, beanbag, balloon, etc.). Adjust the pace so it
      doesn't get dropped too often.

VAR: Play the game with a very slow beat. Use large gestures--keep a steady beat.

VAR: Use a very fast beat. Ss will discover that they have to move closer
      together when there's less time for passing.

29

Tips for <u>ECHOING</u>

This is an immediate-response game. The patterns are somewhat more complex
than previous games.

Explain that you will give a pattern and the Ss are to echo it right back.

Use your judgment about your repeating a pattern. If many students have
not "echoed" accurately, repetition is needed. On the other hand, a few
stragglers will pay better attention if you move ahead with new patterns.

The patterns may involve sounds (snap, clap, stamp, etc.) or actions
(raise one finger, shrug shoulders, bend knees, etc.) or holding a position
through a silent but felt beat (*).

Improvise freely in this game, and encourage the Ss to make up patterns for
the class.

<u>YOUR NOTES</u>

ECHOING

	*	*	*	*
T begins pattern:	(SNAP)	(TOUCH BOTH SHOULDERS)	(SNAP-snap)	(TOUCH BOTH SHOULDERS)
Ss echo softly, keeping the beat:	(SNAP)	(TOUCH BOTH SHOULDERS)	(SNAP-snap)	(TOUCH BOTH SHOULDERS) #
T changes pattern:	(TOUCH HEAD)	(TOUCH BOTH SHOULDERS)	(SNAP-snap)	(TOUCH BOTH SHOULDERS)
Ss echo:	(TOUCH HEAD)	(TOUCH BOTH SHOULDERS)	(SNAP-snap)	(TOUCH BOTH SHOULDERS) #

etc.

The game continues as above with constantly improvised action.

VAR: T's pattern is echoed by individual Ss in turn down a row.

VAR: T calls randomly on individual Ss to echo.

VAR: T selects S to give the pattern for the class to echo.

VAR: Use a word-pattern ("WIN-ter, SPRING, SUM-mer, FALL," etc.)

VAR: Use a phrase (THIRD GRADE, EM-er-son SCHOOL," etc.)

31

Tips for <u>DELAYED ECHO</u>

Explain that you will give a four-beat pattern. Keeping the beat, Ss are
to think it through and then echo it.

Make up your own catchy four-beat patterns; let the Ss improvise too.

DELAYED ECHO

	*	*	*	*
T presents pattern:	(PAT) *(pats knees)*	(CLAP-clap)	(PAT)	(CLAP)
Ss THINK pattern *(no practicing!):*	(*)	(*)	(*)	(*)
Ss echo pattern:	(PAT)	(CLAP-clap)	(PAT)	(CLAP) #
T changes the pattern:	(PAT)	(CLAP)	(TOUCH) *(touches ears)*	(CLAP)
Ss THINK pattern:	(*)	(*)	(*)	(*)
Ss echo pattern:	(PAT)	(CLAP)	(TOUCH)	(CLAP) #

etc.

_____

VAR: Game is played as above, but T indicates in turn which individual Ss
     are to echo.

VAR: S originates the pattern for the class to think, then echo.

VAR: A spoken pattern may be used. Unusual words are fun:

   JADE,   RU-by,   MA-la-chite,   GOLD!

33

LEARNING GAMES

Tips for <u>STOP AND GO</u>

<u>STOP AND GO</u> is an excellent game for teaching traffic safety. Begin with the students standing and be sure to allow enough room for the traffic flow; otherwise, you might have a terrible traffic jam on your hands.

<u>YOUR NOTES</u>

STOP AND GO

	*	*	*	*	
T: Keep the beat with me: *(Ss join in, stepping in place)*	(STEP)	(STEP)	(STEP)	(STEP)	#
When T says STOP, the stepping ceases, but the beat feeling goes on:	(STEP)	(STEP)	(STEP)	STOP<u></u>!	
	(*)	(*)	(*)	(*)	#
When T says GO, the stepping resumes:	(*)	(*)	(*)	GO<u></u>!	
	(STEP)	(STEP)	(STEP)	(STEP)	#
	(STEP)	(STEP)	(STEP)	(STEP)	#
T: Again put the beat in your feet *(Ss step in place)* but I will hold up the red circle to mean <u>STOP</u>.	(STEP)	(STEP)	(STEP)	<u>STOP</u>!	

Now ask the class which color means GO; use a green circle to signal stepping again.

VAR: Set up an imaginary street which students must cross to get to their desks; set a brisk walking beat and have them observe the STOP and GO signals.

VAR: Let a student be the traffic patrol and give the signals.

37

Tips for <u>LOUD AND SOFT I, II, and III</u>

The following three games are useful in reinforcing the concept of loud and
soft. Patterns can be developed to make these games very challenging.
These games can really energize your students. Exaggerating the vocal
projection will make these games more exciting: make the louds very
loud and the softs very soft. Games II and III are extended variations
of Game I.

Note that the fully-capitalized words are to be spoken loudly; the
lower case words are soft.

<u>YOUR NOTES</u>

LOUD AND SOFT I

	*	*	*	*	
T: Here's a pattern for loud and soft.	LOUD	LOUD	LOUD	LOUD	
	soft	soft	soft	soft	#
Now let's say it together *(Ss join in):*	LOUD	LOUD	LOUD	LOUD	
	soft	soft	soft	soft	#
Now let's clap it:	(CLAP)	(CLAP)	(CLAP)	(CLAP)	
	(clap)	(clap)	(clap)	(clap)	#

etc.

VAR: Use a fist on the desk for LOUD and a finger tap for soft. Improvise other contrasts.

VAR: Walk the pattern, stamping for LOUD and tip-toeing for soft.

VAR: Change the pattern, for example: L/s/L/s, etc.

VAR: Change the line to a three-beat pattern: L/s/s, etc.

VAR: Change the line to a five-beat pattern: L/s/s/L/L, etc.

VAR: Divide the class, one half producing the LOUD beats, the other half the soft beats.

39

YOUR NOTES

LOUD AND SOFT II

	*	*	*	*	
T: Listen for my pattern of <u>LOUD</u> and soft. *(Count the beats, reinforcing them with <u>LOUD</u> and soft claps as appropriate.)*	<u>ONE</u>	<u>TWO</u>	Three	Four	
	<u>FIVE</u>	<u>SIX</u>	Seven	Eight	#
Now echo it back to me:	<u>ONE</u>	<u>TWO</u>	Three	Four	
	<u>FIVE</u>	<u>SIX</u>	Seven	Eight	#
On your paper, make <u>BIG</u> marks for <u>LOUD</u>, small for <u>soft</u>.					#

Now write it on your paper
using <u>BIG</u> numbers for <u>LOUD</u>,
small numbers for soft.

etc.

VAR: Change the pattern, for example: L/s/L/s, s/L/s/s, s/L/s/L, L/s/s/s.

VAR: Use <u>LOUD</u>-soft contrasts over a true eight-beat pattern, for example
s/L/<u>L/L</u>/s/L/s/L, etc.

41

YOUR NOTES

LOUD AND SOFT III

		*	*	*	*	
T:	Here's our pattern:	LOUD	soft	LOUD	soft	#

Let's say the days of the
week in that pattern

	MON-day	Tuesday	WEDNES-day	Thurs-day, etc.

Let's say your names in
that pattern:

	ANNE	Bil-ly	TIM	Sus-an, etc.

Now the alphabet:

	A	b	C	d, etc.

_____

VAR: Alternate LOUD and soft lines in saying a familiar poem, for example:

MA-RY   HAD A   LIT-TLE   LAMB.

Its fleece was white   as   snow   (*)

AND EVERY   -   WHERE THAT   MA-RY   WENT

The lamb   was   sure   to   go.   (*)

VAR: Use math facts: 1 + 1 = 2 (LOUD)
                   1 + 2 = 3 (soft)

VAR: Change the pattern, for example: L/s/s, s/L/L/s, etc.

Tips for HIGH AND LOW

Many "opposites" or "contrasts" can be successfully dramatized in a rhythmic game. HIGH AND LOW and its variant NEAR AND FAR are merely examples to spark your own ideas for improvisation.

Use concepts that you want to reinforce with an elementary class, such as left/right, in/out, etc.

YOUR NOTES

HIGH AND LOW

	*	*	*	*

T: Here's a pattern--four beats
HIGH, then four beats low:

HIGH	HIGH	HIGH	HIGH	
low	low	low	low	#

*(T speaks the pattern, emphasizing
high and low with voice)*

Let's say it together:

HIGH	HIGH	HIGH	HIGH	
low	low	low	low	#

Now let's clap it high:

CLAP	CLAP	CLAP	CLAP

Now let's clap it low:

clap	clap	clap	clap	#

*(T and Ss clap on each beat, reaching
up for high and down for low)*

How else could we do that
pattern? If your knees are
HIGH, let the feet be low:

(HIGH)	(HIGH)	(HIGH)	(HIGH)	

(T and Ss touching knees on each beat)

(low)	(low)	(low)	(low)	#

(T and Ss touching feet on each beat)

If your eyes are HIGH, let
your nose be low: *(etc.)*

VAR: Change the pattern: H/l/H/l or l/l/l/H or l/H/H/l, etc.

VAR: Divide the class, one half doing HIGH parts, the other half the low.

VAR: Use NEAR and far as the contrast, clapping or snapping NEAR YOUR EAR,
far from your ear; NEAR THE FLOOR, far from the floor, etc.

Tips for <u>RHYME TIME</u>

<u>RHYME TIME</u> may either introduce or reinforce the rhyming concept.

<u>YOUR NOTES</u>

RHYME TIME

		*	*	*	*	
T taps and says:		TAP	TAP	TAP	TAP	#
T claps and says:		CLAP	CLAP	CLAP	CLAP	#
T snaps and says:		SNAP	SNAP	SNAP	SNAP	#

T: What do you hear that's special about these three words, TAP, CLAP, and SNAP?

Discuss rhyming: *spell the words on the board and show the "AP" in each.*

Ask Ss for more words that rhyme with these three. Put them into a beat pattern. Note that NAP, LAP, and ZAP suggest gestures.

47

Tips for <u>YOU RHYME</u>

With <u>YOU RHYME</u>, it is not necessary for each word to have an associated gesture. The clapping makes a structure for the timing of response.

<u>YOUR NOTES</u>

YOU RHYME

*   *   *   *

T: Let's make some other
     rhymes. Bill, let's
     start with you and go
     down your row. Every-
     body clap and I'll give
     the first word.   (CLAP)   (CLAP)   (CLAP)   BALL!
                                    (teacher)

                               (CLAP)   (CLAP)   (CLAP)   TALL!
                                (Bill's rhyme)

                               (CLAP)   (CLAP)   (CLAP)   FALL!
                                (Ann's rhyme)

Begin a new word when you run out of rhymes. Try "High" next (try, cry, my, sky, pie, etc.)

VAR: For a faster game,
       use fewer claps: STICK   (CLAP)   THICK   (CLAP) etc.
                       (teacher)   *(student)*

VAR: For an even faster
       game, use no claps: EAT   NEAT   FOG   DOG
                    (teacher) *(student)* *(teacher)* *(student)*

Tips for <u>ACTION RHYME</u>

In <u>ACTION RHYME</u> the word to be rhymed is given first, followed by the appropriate gesture on the next three beats. The selected rhyming word is then followed by its own gesture for three beats.

<u>YOUR NOTES</u>

ACTION RHYME

	*	*	*	*	
T begins game by saying:	TOP!	(*)	(*)	(*)	#
	(taps top of head on each beat)			*(as needed)*	
Pre-selected S responds:	HOP!	(HOP)	(HOP)	(HOP)	#
	(S acts out own response)				
Another S responds:	MOP!	(MOP)	(MOP)	(MOP)	#
	(S acts out own response)				
				etc.	

———————————————

VAR: Encourage creative beat-keeping. Ss can fill out the beat pattern
with appropriate words, for example:

BEE!	BUZZ	BUZZ	BUZZ
SINGING!	LAH-dee	DAH-dee	DAH

VAR: Use a phrase: BRING-ing YOU   a BAS   -   KET

51

Tips for <u>RHYMING RIDDLES</u>

<u>RHYMING RIDDLES</u> is a guessing game in pantomime.

<u>YOUR NOTES</u>

RHYMING RIDDLES

		*	*	*	*
T:	Who can guess this rhyme?	(BLINK)	(BLINK)	(BLINK)	(BLINK)
	T touches head:	(TOUCH)	(TOUCH)	(TOUCH)	(TOUCH)

ANSWER: BLINK/THINK

	Here's another one:	(POINT)	(POINT)	(POINT)	(POINT)
		(T points to eye)			
	T makes flying motions:	(FLAP)	(FLAP)	(FLAP)	(FLAP)

ANSWER: EYE/FLY

_____

VAR: Ask for S volunteers to present a rhyming pair of words.

Tips for <u>BASIC SHAPES</u>

This is an excellent game for introducing such basic geometric patterns as the line, circle, triangle, square, and rectangle. As you can see, quite a bit of classroom space is required, so be sure to plan ahead. Emphasize circles and straight lines especially, as these form the foundation for playing the next game, <u>SHAPES OF LETTERS</u>.

This game and the one following come from the eurhythmic exercises employed in workshops conducted by Robert Abramson of the Manhattan School of Music.

<u>YOUR NOTES</u>

BASIC SHAPES

T: Let's make a straight line with people. I'll give you TEN COUNTS to make
a straight line with your classmates--no touching! Help me count.

```
     *     *     *     *     *     *     *     *     *     *
                                                              STRAIGHT
     1     2     3     4     5     6     7     8     9    10   LINE
                                                              (shouted)
                                         *     *     *     *
Now we will step in place,
keeping the line straight:              (STEP) (STEP) (STEP) (STEP)    #

Now you can break the line and
walk wherever you like--but keep
the beat in your feet:                  (WALK) (WALK) (WALK) (WALK)    #

Now we'll take six counts to
make a straight line again. (etc.)
```

_____

VAR: In similar fashion, form a circle, triangle, square, rectangle, etc.

VAR: Ask for smaller groups ("With three other people, make a square.")

VAR: Let the arms be used to make the shape.

VAR: Use the ten-count procedure (as above) to make two straight lines,
girls in one and boys in the other.

Tips for <u>SHAPES OF LETTERS</u>

After <u>BASIC SHAPES</u> has been mastered, you are ready to form all
twenty-six letters of the alphabet. Fifteen letters require straight
lines only; eight are formed with a combination of straight and curved
lines, and only three letters require curved lines exclusively.

Encourage the students to notice the emerging shape and to adjust their
positions without touching and without talking. Again, this game requires
classroom space.

<u>YOUR NOTES</u>

SHAPES OF LETTERS

	*	*	*	*
T says:	EIGHT	COUNTS to the	SHAPE of an	A!
	HERE	WE	GO!	(*)
	ONE,	TWO,	THREE,	FOUR,
	FIVE,	SIX,	SEV-en,	EIGHT - A!

(class shouts)

VAR: Experiment with all the letters over a period of time. Some are
easy (O, C, X) and some are difficult.

VAR: T says, "This time, let's make two A's--everyone wearing blue over
here, those not wearing blue over there."

VAR: Vary the number of counts and/or their speed. Fewer counts or a
faster pace requires a quicker student response.

VAR: Use STEPS for COUNTS. This requires some thought and much more
control on everyone's part.

VAR: Use the shapes of numbers.

Tips for <u>MISSISSIPPI SPELLER</u>

This is not really a game, but a memory device for spelling help.
Remember the familiar chant for spelling "Mississippi"? Chant
troublesome spelling words to a beat to foster total student involvement

Here's some more old-fashioned spelling advice set to a beat:

      *   *   *   *

     I   be-fore E   ex - CEPT af-ter C

or SOUND-ed as A, as in   NEIGH-bor or WEIGH

<u>YOUR NOTES</u>

THE MISSISSIPPI SPELLER

T introduces the chant, snapping or clapping on each beat:

```
     *                   *                   *                   *

M                   I                   CROOK-ed let-ter   CROOK-ed let-ter

I              CROOK-ed let-ter   CROOK-ed let-ter        I

HUMP  -  back      HUMP  -  back           I                   (*)
```

Ss imitate, repeating without breaking the beat until it becomes easy.

Change to taps, nods, stamps, etc., without breaking the beat.

VAR: Sometimes a rhyming jingle helps, for example:

```
     *                   *                   *                   *

im - POR - tant   to    YOU,          im - POR - tant   to    ME--

    I   -  m  -   P  -  o  -  r  -  T  -  a  -  n  -  T
```

```
         *               *               *               *

         P   - e-    O   -    P   -l-   E

         IT'S    as    EA-sy    AS    can    BE!
```

Tips for <u>LETTER BEATS</u>

This game will reinforce recognizing the letters of the alphabet, both in and out of sequence.

Begin with large, readable letters placed in alphabetical order on a felt board, chalkboard or bulletin board.

Keep the beat very steady. An uneven or lagging beat hinders concentration and efficient memorizing.

<u>YOUR NOTES</u>

LETTER BEATS

```
                        *            *            *            *

T says:                 AL - pha BET,   AL - pha BET,

                        ALL    the LET - ters  IN    a    ROW.

                        AL - pha BET,   AL - pha BET,

                        SAY    it  WITH me,   HERE   we   GO!
T points to each letter
as Ss speak:            A            B            C            D  etc.
```

_____

VAR: Notice which letters are least familiar to the Ss. Drill on each one
      separately for recognition, using a steady beat.

```
                        Q            Q            Q            Q  etc.
```

VAR: Alternate difficult letters out of sequence using a steady beat:

```
                        M            W,           M            W  etc.
```

VAR: Leave the alphabet in sequence in the board, but take out some letters,
      leaving space where they belong. Ask Ss to speak the letters seen and
      clap for the missing letters:

```
                        A          (CLAP)     (CLAP)          D  etc.
```

VAR: Reverse the above procedure by clapping for the letters seen and speaking
      the missing letters. (In the example below, A and D are seen.)

```
                        (CLAP)       B            C          (CLAP) etc.
```

VAR: Use short segments of the alphabet with missing letters and treat as above.

VAR: When the order is quite familiar, dispense with the visual aids. Ss
      speak the letters from memory with a fast beat, very fast beat, very
      slow beat, etc.

61

Tips for GOING, GOING, GONE

The importance of the silent beat is emphasized by this game. The Ss
must be attentive in order to remember which beats to clap and which
beats remain silent.

The first time you play this game, it can be helpful to show the four-
beat pattern on the board:

                     1   2   3   4

Clap and count this several times. Then erase the number "4" and show
the Ss an open-hand gesture for the silent beat. Reinforce each line
as needed, erasing numbers in sequence. Then play the game as a whole.

This game comes from the eurhythmic exercises employed in workshops
conducted by Robert Abramson of the Manhattan School of Music.

GOING, GOING, GONE

	*	*	*	*
T: Clap and speak with me:	1	2	3	4
Show each silent beat with a gesture:	1	2	3	(*)
	1	2	(*)	(*)
	1	(*)	(*)	(*)
	(*)	(*)	(*)	(*)
Whisper:	ALL	GONE.		

Now let's reverse the game.
Where have all the beats gone?
(Show each beat)

	(*)	(*)	(*)	(*)
	(*)	(*)	(*)	4
	(*)	(*)	3	4
	(*)	2	3	4
	1	2	3	4
	ALL	HERE!		

VAR: This can also be an action game. Play it in a circle with a STEP for the existing counts and no-step for the missing counts, replacing the CLAP and no-clap.

VAR: Extend the game to eight counts.

VAR: Use a poem or song, dropping syllables in sequence.

VAR: Use any number or alphabet sequence that needs reinforcement.

Tips for <u>MATH BEATS</u>

This game facilitates learning basic math facts. The framework of steady beats organizes the students' problem-solving response. The rhythmic repetition is also a strong memory aid.

With some classes, you may want to do a preliminary chant to get the beat going, something like:

        *   *   *   *

    MATH   FACTS,   MATH   FACTS,

    YOU can LEARN   MATH   FACTS!

Start a slower beat if the students have difficulty responding in rhythm. When they know the tables well, use a crisp, quick beat.

<u>YOUR NOTES</u>

MATH BEATS

		*	*	*	*
T:	Let's do the "one-pluses." Here's the beat:	(TAP)	(TAP)	(TAP)	(TAP)
	Now tap with me:	(TAP)	(TAP)	(TAP)	(TAP)	#
	Say it together now:	1 +	1	=	2
	(tapping continues)	1 +	2	=	3

etc.

VAR: T alone supplies first part of equation, Ss respond with the sum.

VAR: T supplies first part of equation, individual Ss answer in turn.

VAR: For quicker thinking, play the game with only three beats:

	*	*	*
	11 +	1 =	12

etc.

VAR: Use subtraction, multiplication, and division tables.

Tips for <u>COLOR CIRCLE</u>

This game needs space. Students form one large circle or several smaller
circles. Each student wears a card with a color dot on one side and
the spelled-out color name on the other. Use primary colors (red,
yellow, blue), secondary colors (orange, green, purple), or a combination.

<u>YOUR NOTES</u>

COLOR CIRCLE

*	*	*	*

T sets beat by saying: ROUND - a - BOUT and ROUND - a - BOUT and

Ss join in and walk around ROUND - a - BOUT we GO!   (*)
in a circle, taking a step
on each beat: WHEN   WILL we STOP,   DOES

  AN - y BO - dy KNOW?   (*)   #

(Repeat as needed)

T calls out "STOP!" and gives instructions, for instance:

- Five counts for all "REDS" to sit down. *(Everyone else remains standing.)*

- Eight counts for "YELLOWS" to make pairs.

- With your eyes, find someone with a BLUE dot. Ten slow counts for everybody
  to stand close to a "BLUE."

- If your color means "BE CAREFUL" (or "STOP" or "GO"), three counts to go
  to the middle of the circle. *(T relates colors to traffic lights.)*

- Eight counts for each "RED" and "YELLOW" pair to capture an "ORANGE."
  (Oranges are captured by one red and one yellow in "London Bridge" fashion.
  This activity is excellent for reinforcing the secondary-color concept.)

VARS: Reverse the cards to show the color words (same activities as above).
       Use half color dots/half color words: "Ten counts to find your match."
       Use colors of Ss' clothing instead of cards.

Tips for <u>POCKET MONEY</u>

Learning to count money is easier when the value units are visualized as in this game. We recommend that you try this warm-up activity before playing <u>POCKET MONEY</u>: with the students sitting in a circle, chant the first four lines of the verse, repeating as needed; then repeat with the Ss standing, stepping the beat in place. Now you are ready to play <u>POCKET MONEY</u>.

<u>YOUR NOTES</u>

POCKET MONEY

T: Pretend that each one of you is a penny. Walk around in the circle and say with me:

           *   *

PEN-nies   in   a   POCK-et,

PEN-nies   in   a   POCK-et,

PEN-nies   in   a   POCK-et,

ONE   cent   EACH.   #
_____

LET'S   make   NICK-els,

LET'S   make   NICK-els,

LET'S   make   NICK-els,

FIVE   cents   EACH.

T counts off Ss, forming groups of 5 who join hands in small circles. The game continues:

ONE   TWO   THREE   FOUR   FIVE: #

NICK-els   in   a   POCK-et,

NICK-els   in   a   POCK-et,

NICK-els   in   a   POCK-et,

FIVE   cents   EACH.

Counting up: after you have made nickles or dimes (as above), count up the change by the coins you have made. If you have made nickles with 28 students, count up as follows: "5 - 10 - 15 - 20 - 25 with three pennies left over-- that equals 28 cents."
_____

VAR: Each student is a penny; make dimes or quarters.
       Each student is a nickel; make dimes, quarters or half-dollars.
       Each student is a dime; make half dollars and dollars.

69

Tips for <u>THE CLOCK</u>

This simple game stresses the steady-beat concept through pendulum-like motions. Note the suggestion for varying the size of the gestures to imitate small and large clocks.

<u>YOUR NOTES</u>

THE CLOCK

.

         *   *   *   *

T begins pendulum gestures
and says: TICK   TOCK   TICK   TOCK

                     TICK   TOCK   TICK   TOCK   #

Ss join and imitate.   *etc.*

VAR: Use tiny gestures for a small clock ticking softly, and big gestures
       for a grandfather clock ticking loudly.

Tips for <u>AROUND THE CLOCK</u>

<u>AROUND THE CLOCK</u> introduces to the students the idea of clockwise and counter-clockwise motion. Have the students form a circle with everyone holding hands. With everyone saying "Tick-Tock," have the students step to the beat in a clockwise direction:

After the beat has been firmly established, T signals changing the direction of the circle to counter-clockwise:

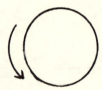

T can alternate at will the clockwise and counter-clockwise direction of the circle after the Ss are comfortable with the basic concept.

<u>YOUR NOTES</u>

AROUND THE CLOCK

	*	*	*	*	

Ss (holding hands in a circle)
step clockwise to the beat
and say:

TICK	TOCK	TICK	TOCK	#

After beat and motion are well-
established, T changes the
direction of the circle by
saying:

TICK	TOCK,	COUNT-er	CLOCK-wise!

TICK	TOCK	TICK	TOCK	#

T changes the circle to clock-
wise direction by saying:

TICK	TOCK,	CLOCK	-	WISE!

etc.

VAR: Use tiny steps for a small clock (ticking softly) and big steps for
a large clock (ticking loudly).

VAR: Use TICK-TOCK for clockwise motion, TOCK-TICK for counter-clockwise
motion.

Tips for TELLING TIME

TELLING TIME enables the student to be physically part of a moving clock. This game can be used to introduce or to review telling time.

Twelve (12) numbered Ss stand in a circle as a clock face. One student represents the little hand, standing in the middle of the circle, extending his/her arms and putting the hands together to form the arrow.

The big hand is an arrow taped to the floor pointing to the 12.

The remaining Ss, outlining the clock face, form a circle around the numbered students.

YOUR NOTES

TELLING TIME

		*	*	*	*	
T begins game by saying:		TICK	TOCK	TICK	TOCK	#
Ss join in:		TICK	TOCK	TICK	TOCK	#
T indicates desired time:		TICK	TOCK	<u>FIVE</u>	O CLOCK	#
		TICK	TOCK	TICK	TOCK	#

etc.

Keep the clock ticking while the "little hand" finds the correct number.
The "little hand" should always move clockwise, stepping to the steady
beat. Ss take turns being the "little hand."

VAR: This game can be adapted for telling more exact time (the half-hour,
quarter-hours, etc.) by allowing another S to be the "big hand."

Tips for <u>GROUPING</u>

Grouping is a fundamental concept for the elementary classroom. There's almost no end to the adaptations of this game and the ones following it. Suggested here are ways to rhythmicize color recognition (including how to make secondary colors) and number recognition (including some math reinforcement).

You may use the initial game, <u>GROUPING</u>, to help introduce the basic concept. Consider employing it to assist in assembling your reading or math groups. Clap until each student has found his/her place. You may use <u>GROUPING</u> to precede any other grouping game.

Exact words really don't matter with these games. Improvise freely, but always keep the beat steady. Part of the fun is keeping the beat even with lots of syllables:

      *   *   *   *

    JOHN-ny, you're a BLUE;   go   OV-er there with SUE.

<u>YOUR NOTES</u>

GROUPING

*   *   *   *

T, clapping on each
beat, says: GROUP- ing's USE - ful, GROUP - ing's FUN.

            THERE'S a GROUP for EV - ery ONE!

            FORM your GROUP, WALK don't RUN

Ss join clapping: and CLAP,   CLAP,   EV- - ery ONE

            (*) un - TIL your GROUP - ing's DONE! #

                          etc.

Tips for <u>ANYBODY WEARING GREEN?</u>

When the Ss respond to your questioning, help them shape their answers so
the words fall rhythmically with the established beat. It does not matter
how many or how few clapped beats occur between your question and its
answer.

<u>YOUR NOTES</u>

ANYBODY WEARING GREEN?

	*	*	*	*
T starts by asking this question, keeping the beat while everybody claps:	Is AN-y bo-dy	WEAR - ing	GREEN	to - DAY?
	Is AN-y bo-dy	WEAR - ing	GREEN?	(*)
	IF you're	WEAR - ing	GREEN	to - DAY
	GO to the	FRONT and	FORM a	LINE,
Continue clapping as the green group is formed. Then the game proceeds with the T saying:	EV'ry body	WEAR - ing	GREEN.	(*)
	(CLAP)	(CLAP)	(CLAP)	(CLAP) #
	(*)	(*)	(*)	NOW
	TELL us	WHERE your	GREEN	IS.
	BOB?	(CLAP)	(CLAP)	(CLAP)

(Ss clap until Bob is ready to answer)

My SHIRT is	GREEN.	(*)	(*)

(Bob answers)

KA - ren?	(*)	GREEN	RIB-bon.

(Karen answers)

T may point to individuals:	GREEN	JEANS,	GREEN	EYES.

(Dick answers)   *(Pam answers)*

etc.

---

	*	*	*	*
VAR: Let the response for each color be different:	EV'ry body	WEAR - ing	BLUE,	PLEASE stand
	UP!	(*)	(*)	(*)
	EV'ry body	WEAR - ing	RED,	RAISE your
	HAND!	(*)	(*)	(*)

etc.

Tips for <u>COLOR CARDS</u>

To begin this game, each S is given a large color card (8-1/2 x 11 is highly visible). The cards may be held in front of the chest by hand, or hung from the neck with yarn or string.

<u>YOUR NOTES</u>

COLOR CARDS

	*	*	*	*	
T sets beat with the following phrase, Ss clapping along:	ALL the REDS	come O-ver		HERE.	
Ss echo each verbal direction and make groups as directed:	ALL the REDS	come O-ver		HERE.	
Clap until REDS are grouped:	(*)	(*)	(*)	(*)	#
T now says:	IF you're BLUE,	O-ver		THERE.	
Ss echo:	IF you're BLUE,	O-ver		THERE.	
Clap until BLUES are formed:	(*)	(*)	(*)	(*)	#
T now says:	YEL-lows, GO to the	DOOR	-	WAY.	
Ss echo:	YEL-lows, GO to the	DOOR	-	WAY.	
Clap until YELLOWS are formed:	(*)	(*)	(*)	(*)	#

etc.

VAR: Grouping can be used to show how to make secondary colors. Calculate the
cards passed out so that for every orange, there is one red card and one
yellow card. Likewise, for purple and green. Explain that this game is
a bit like "London Bridge."

TELL me HOW	to	MAKE	PUR-ple.
BLUE and RED		MAKE	PUR-ple.
BLUES and REDS,		CAP-ture a	PUR-ple.

etc.

VAR: Cards may spell out the color names.

Tips for PEOPLE-GROUPING

In this game, Ss form themselves into groups of varying number according to the teacher's direction. Begin by making pairs, as outlined; then call for groups of 5, 8, etc. You need not proceed in numerical order. In forming the larger groups especially, each S develops judgment in assessing his/her role in a fluid numerical situation.

Students are standing to begin the game. Allow them space to move.

YOUR NOTES

	*	*	*	*
T calls for forming groups:	LET'S	GROUP	by TWO'S	NOW.
T claps as Ss respond:	(CLAP)	(CLAP)	(CLAP)	(CLAP) #
T then says:	NOW count OFF:		ONE,	TWO;

(Ss count off within group)

ONE,	TWO;	ONE,	TWO; #

etc.

VAR: Change the number of Ss contained in each group. Remember to have the Ss count off within each group after the groups are formed, to check their counting accuracy. T can vary the wording which calls groups to form (see below). Always keep the beat steady, clapping while the groups form.

To form groups of five:	LET'S	MAKE	FIVES	NOW, etc.
To form groups of eight:	PUT	EIGHT in	EV-ery	GROUP, etc.
To form groups of twelve:	THIS	TIME,	TWELVE in a	GROUP, etc.

Remaining Ss should be counted too:

	THREE	GROUPS of	SEV-en	EACH,
or	HOW	MA-ny	LEFT	OV-er?
	WHAT'S	THE	re- MAIN -	DER?

83

Tips for KNOW YOUR NUMBER

Large cards displaying the numbers you want to emphasize are passed out in random order, one to each student. As with the game COLOR CARDS, these numbered cards may be held in the hands, hung, or pinned to the students.

YOUR NOTES

<u>KNOW YOUR NUMBER</u>

T gives verbal directions,   *   *   *   *
allowing enough clapped time
to let Ss respond before the
direction is changed: ALL   the   THREES,   RAISE   your   HANDS.

(CLAP)   (CLAP)   (CLAP)   (CLAP)   #

SE-vens,   PUT   your   HEAD   DOWN.

(CLAP)   (CLAP)   (CLAP)   (CLAP)   #

ZE-ro,   MAKE   an   "O"   (*)
                                    (thumb and forefinger)

(CLAP)   (CLAP)   (CLAP)   (CLAP)   #
                                                etc.

VAR: You can reinforce math processes with this game:

GROUP   SO   your   SUM   is   TEN, etc.

VAR: Prepare half the cards with Arabic numerals and the other half with the
      numbers spelled out. Then:

EIGHT   COUNTS   to   FIND   your   MATCH:

ONE,   TWO,   THREE,   FOUR, etc.

A REMINDER

You may have been pacing these games at a rather medium speed, not fast, not slow. Try FAST! Try s l o w . . . These changes are remarkably refreshing.

AN ENCOURAGEMENT

Everything we now teach as organized, "given" knowledge was once a discovery (yes, even such mundane things as 2 + 2 = 4). The organization of such knowledge helps to make it memorable.

Just so, each game in this handbook was once an improvisation, taking its printed form only after quite a bit of experimentation. But the printed form is not a definitive form, only one place to begin. We have tried to show you how flexible and open-ended these eurhythmic processes are by suggesting some variations. Many variants will occur to you; they are legitimate and you can follow them wherever their implications lead you.

The basic process might be called RHYTHMICIZING: making use of that almost magical response human beings have to a steady pulse to guide intellectual and physical responses.

You and your students are encouraged to notice and to explore rhythmicizing processes beyond the boundaries of this handbook.